Hummingbirds: How to Attract and Feed with a Backyard Habitat

By: Brian Grant

Published by:

Brian Grant and Random Technologies
4409 HOFFNER AVENUE, 347
Belle Isle, FL 32812

Sign up for more fascinating information about wild birds at:
www.attractingwildbirds.com

Table of Contents

The History and Habits of Hummingbirds

A lot of people know what a hummingbird looks like. Their bright colors, combined with their size, make them a distinctive little bird. Some of the key features that identify a hummingbird may include: the length of its tongue, its bill, the tiny size of its wings, or their nonpasserine nature.

That being said, there's a lot more to the Trochilidae. Don't recognize the name? Trochilidae is the name that has been given to describe the 323 species of hummingbirds.

The fact that there are 323 distinct species of hummingbird represents a substantially less known fact about the hummingbird, and just one of the many fascinating discoveries of this "jewel of the sky" that you're going to learn by reading this guide.

History of the Hummingbird

So where have hummingbirds come from? What do they do? What are their habits?

The information that we have so far about this fascinating species has lead researchers to believe that they first appeared in the Northern Andes Mountains (of South America).

They haven't stayed there though as they have spread throughout the Western Hemisphere.

The hot zones for hummingbirds include Columbia, Ecuador, and Peru, but they've been found as far north as Alaska to as far south Chile.

How many species are in…

- Colombia, Ecuador, and Peru?
- Costa Rica?
- United States?

100, 50, 16 Respectively

Hummingbirds and the Ecosystem

Hummingbirds are known for several of their habits. We've already discussed their distinctive size, but they are also known for their tremendous abilities with flight, and for the fact that they are actually a vital part of any ecosystem they join.

This vitality comes from the hummingbird's taste for nectar. Hummingbirds collect nectar for themselves, but end up benefiting the ecosystem around them by collecting pollen at the same time. As they then travel from flower to flower they end up pollinating the surrounding plants. Pollination then helps the plant reproduce, and thus helps the ecosystem to thrive.

That being said, nectar is not all that hummingbirds eat. These tiny little creatures eat small insects of any variety. They have various strategies to get more access to insects, including darting together with other hummingbirds or flitting from perch to perch. These smaller creatures provide the rest of the necessary vitamins, minerals and protein to round out the diet of the hummingbird.

Flight Patterns of the Hummingbird

Hummingbirds are also known for their distinct patterns of flight, often thought to resemble letters. North Americans frequently class these flight patterns by the letter, denoting a J, O, or U shaped flight as they watch these curious creatures.

Interestingly, there is method to the madness here, and hummingbird flight patterns are not accidental. They seem to be designed to maximize male exposure to sunlight. This may sound insignificant, but it really contributes to the males' ability to display bright gorget – the term given to describe the bright feathers they need to attract a mate.

Migration Patterns

Several species of hummingbirds do not like the cold, and in fact cannot survive in it. Their diet of nectar and insects necessitates a warm climate, regardless of the season. For that reason, several species are either settled near the Ecuador, or have adapted over time.

North American hummers are the only ones that can survive the cold. Their feathers often allow them to tolerate cold for hours – a few days. That being said, they too will perish if they do not migrate within that time.

Songs of the Hummingbird

Hummingbirds don't sing in the traditional sense, their song is a variety of chips, chatter, chits and whistles. It is their wings that make the humming sound, the only hummingbird species that's known to really sound like traditional bird song is the buff bellied hummingbird.

Amazing Creatures

All in all, the hummingbird is a remarkable animal. They help pollination, fly in patterns, and controls its bodily demand for resources when it's trying to survive.

That being said, there are several hundred species of variation even within the hummingbird family. These species can sometimes differ in their abilities, appearance, and location, but all share the same genetic origin – believed to be somewhere from the Andes.

Attracting Hummingbirds to Your Garden

Attracting hummingbirds to your garden is as simple as ensuring you have a feeder with the right type of sustenance to keep your hummers happy. It's a hobby with a high degree of reward, and a relatively low amount of maintenance. The biggest investment is the start-up in selecting the feeder that's best for you.

Selecting a Feeder

Feeders come in a variety of different sizes and materials, and not every feeder is going to be best for you. By taking the time to look at what's on the market, you can be sure you do not have to replace your feeder every year because it broke, and instead have a lasting and rewarding experience.

Best feeder materials

A good feeder should be built to last. While cheap plastic feeders may seem initially more attractive, they actually break a lot easier (particularly in the heat), and often need replacing. Other types of feeders may well be worth the additional cost.

The best types of feeders are made out of sturdy plastic and weighted glass. These will last, and they aren't nearly as brittle as the cheap plastic ones on the market (trust me, you can tell the difference). Ultimately it's your call, just keep in mind the investment that will come with continually replacing a feeder – a good one should be able to last you for years to come!

Types of Feeders

The main types of feeders are dish feeders and bottle feeders. As the names suggest, dish feeders offer a covered plate type feeding experience, whereas bottle feeders hang a little higher like a bottle, with food dispensers around it.

Each type has its advantage and disadvantage, and either will work, it's just a decision you'll need to make. Some people will tell you "this way is the only way to go" or "that way!" but the truth is that both have their place in the world of hummers.

Dish feeders are shallow, so they only hold about 16 ounces of food. On the other hand, bottle feeders can leak, causing waste of food. It's all up to your preference to decide which risk is worth taking.

Nectar Recipe

Once you've got your feeder, it's time to mix up some food. The following recipe is simple, but reliable and the hummers will love it.

¼ cup of cane sugar mixed with 1 cup water

Bring water to the boil.

Remove from heat and add sugar.

Stir until completely dissolved, cover and let cool.

Store in fridge for up to 5 days.

Simple right? Indeed it is. You can mix up as much as you need, and there's really no need to get fancy here. Just mix the food and keep it fresh! That being said, there are a few things you must avoid.

- Using artificial sugar or sweeteners, honey, or molasses. These ingredients may seem like they'd be good, but really just add complications to the process. The honey, artificial sugar, and molasses that we eat is not the same (at all!) as what the birds would naturally find in the wild. The chemical makeup of other types of sweeteners is not the same as pure cane sugar and can cause sickness and even death to a hummingbird. They burn enormous amounts of energy for their size and need real cane sugar (or even better, a pesticide-free flower garden – details below). Keep it simple and the birds will love it.

- Food coloring. Some people get fancy and dye their foods, however this is merely unnecessary chemical additions to the process.

- Mold. If you wait longer than four days to change the feeder food, you risk developing mold. Since this will harm the birds and ruin the feeder, it's best to change the feed every few days.

The other option for feeding the birds involves ensuring that the little insects they like to eat are in high supply in the yard. This can be done by simply placing an overripe banana there, and watching the flies cluster to it. That being said, sticking with sugar water is going to serve just fine if you don't want to fill sections of the yard with small bugs.

Cleaning the feeder

On top of changing the food every few days, the feeder may need a cleaning at the same time. Make sure the dispenser gets soaked in a mild cleaning solution while you prepare to refill it. This is an easy way to ensure the food stays free from mold and debris and to keep the birds who visit safe.

If you're having trouble reaching sections of the feeder, use a Q-tip to spread the solution. Just don't forget to rinse the cleaning products off, as evidently the chemicals can be harmful to the little guys.

Where should I put my feeder?

Feeders should be hung where they are easy to see, but hard to catch. This allows you to enjoy viewing them in the yard, and to monitor their situations, but it also prevents them from being captured by their natural predators such as feral cats, wild dogs and predatory birds.

Another piece of advice relates to having multiple feeders. If you have more than one feeder, try to keep them out of sight of one another if possible. Hummingbirds are territorial and this will ensure they can separate out a little more.

How can I make it more comfortable for the hummers?

This is a great question, and one not everybody thinks about. The main answers to this come in two forms: perches, and feeders.

Hummingbirds love a twig perch to scope out the place they're going to eat before they try. The other benefit here is that perches can encourage the birds to stop while they're eating. This may be restful for them, but it really helps you to get a good look easier (they're fast little guys otherwise!). All in all, this can really add to the enjoyment of the hobby.

The other thing you can do is to have more than one feeder. Sometimes a single bird gets territorial and attempts to protect its food source. This can be easily circumvented by simply having more than one feeder in your yard, which will discourage bullying.

How Many Birds will Visit?

Different feeders attract different numbers of visitors, but the bottom line is really capacity. How much food does your feeder hold? How much does it need to hold? How many birds can be fed at one time with multiple feeder ports? You'll see this when you note how many hummingbirds are visiting on a regular basis, less birds should equal less feed...and vice versa.

Taking Care of the Hummers who Visit

Being responsible. Hummingbirds are amazing, and they can be a delight to watch, but it's important to remember that they're fragile living creatures. When you set up a feeder, you are potentially teaching them to rely on this source, so don't be inconsistent about feeding and cleaning them. Make sure you're regularly providing fresh food, particularly near times of frost when the birds struggle to find their normal sources.

That in mind, enjoy your little guests! If you feed them, they will come!

Using a Garden to Attract Friends

Many people try to plant flowers to attract hummingbirds to their yard. Sometimes a feeder just isn't cutting it, and if you want more houseguests it may be time to start thinking about what you're planting. There's a variety of plants that hummingbirds love, and this is another great way to attract them.

All you need is a little research, and some planting, and voila!

What Hummingbirds are in your Area?

To begin, it's helpful to understand what types of hummingbirds are found in your area. If you don't know off the top of your head (most of us don't) feel free to consult a local bird watching society, gardening club, or even the library to find out the species of birds in your area. This information can help you to know what seasons are going to work best, and what plants your hummingbirds will prefer, to get your yard full in no time.

When are Hummingbirds Around your Area?

This will depend on the species that are around, but in many parts of the United States there are hummingbirds living year round. The key here is just knowing whether that's the case, or whether there's only particular seasons for them, as this will help you to understand your rates of success.

Which Plants Should be Present?

This is going to vary somewhat, but there is a lot of common ground in the types of plants that hummingbirds enjoy. We're going to provide a specific list a little later in the chapter, based by region, but for now we'll begin with a general discussion.

First, it's interesting to note that hummingbirds don't actually have a strong sense of smell. The garden can smell any way you'd like it to, but it won't have any effect on hummingbird visits. These fun little creatures are apparently curious enough on their own that Mother Nature saw no need to force the attraction between them and plants. Similarly, although there has been some suggestion that they love red or pink flowers best, hummingbirds are really not all that selective. They will pollinate just about any type, and this is good for both them and the garden. The key is to offer variety, and to keep your little garden growing.

Trees and shrubs

We begin with trees and shrubs because this is likely the first step for most gardeners. These can seem like quite the initial investment, often requiring more money and time than smaller flowers, but they can pay off both in beauty and in hummers' interest.

The main thing to keep in mind with trees and shrubs is design. Once they're placed, you're unlikely to move them, so take some time and think about how and where you'd like to position your new plants.

As a bonus, trees and shrubs can also offer places for the birds to nest if they so desire, so it may really be an addition to your new hobby.

Please make note not to trim trees too often if so. And especially reduce tree trimming during migration and breeding season – as the hummingbirds nest are extremely small to see and could be at risk from tree trimming while they are nesting.

Flowers

Flowers are the makings of any garden, let alone one to attract hummingbirds. Use the list that follows later in the chapter to select the best flowers for your desired birds and fill the garden with a variety of them.

Another tip with flowers is to cluster color, as it's both aesthetically pleasing, and attractive to the hummingbirds.

Vines

Vines can be another great addition to the garden, particularly ones that flower and climb. This can also act as an easy way to separate one feeder from another, to prevent territorialism from taking over with the birds.

Please Avoid Pesticides!

It is best to use a natural pesticide alternatives wherever possible, or none at all. The poisonous chemicals have been shown to be the major cause of loss of other pollinators like the honey bee and monarch butterfly. These toxins are also affecting hummingbirds due to their small, fragile bodies. As a bonus of eliminating harmful pesticides from your garden, you may also experience better health too as the same toxic chemicals found in many pesticides contain cancer-causing ingredients.

Additional Touches for the Garden

On top of plants, you can always add birdbaths, fountains, ponds, any source of water to your garden. On top of adding to the natural beauty of the area, hummingbirds also enjoy water, mainly for bathing.

Hummingbirds naturally get their drinking water from the nectar they ingest, but no amount of nectar can help them to feel clean. They enjoy flitting about in shallow water regularly, so this additional touch can really help them to feel comfortable.

Plants by Region

With all of that said, it's time to consider the specific plants that will grow best in your region. Consider the following lists when designing your garden, remembering you don't have to have all of the plants – but variety helps!

Flowers:

Autumn sage
Anise sage
Bee balm or bergamot
Bleeding heart
Butterfly weed
Canna lily
Cardinal flower
Chuparosa
Columbine
Coral Bells
Daylily
Delphinium or scarlet larkspur
Four o'clock
Foxglove
Fuchsia
Gladiolus
Hollyhock
Hosta or plantain lily
Hummingbird trumpet
Hyssop
Jewelweed or spotted jewelweed
Mexican milkweed
Mexican sunflower
Nasturtium
Penstemons or beardtongue
Phlox
Pineapple sage
Red-hot poker or tritoma
Scarlet gilia or skyrocket
Scarlet sage or red salvia
Snapdragon
Spider flower
Standing cypress
Texas sage
Zinnia

Vines:

Coral or trumpet honeysuckle
Cross vine
Cypress vine
Firecracker vine
Mexican flame vine
Red morning glory
Scarlet runner bean
Trumpet creeper

Shrubs:

Azalea
Beauty bush
Bottlebrush
Butterfly bush
Crimson-flowering currant
Flame acanthus
Flowering quince
Hardy fuchsia
Hibiscus
Lantana
Lilac
Manzanita
Red buckeye
Shrimp plant
Snowberry
Sultan's turban
Turk's cap
Weigela or cardinal shrub

Trees:

Buckeye
Black locust
Citrus
Flowering crab-apple
Hawthorn
Mimosa or silk tree
Red horse chestnut
Siberian pea tree
Tulip poplar

Alternatives to Pesticides

In the last chapter we discussed the importance of avoiding chemical pesticides. This does not mean that we want your garden overrun with pests, this means looking for alternative solutions to dealing with pests. The solution you select will depend on the type of pest, so we're going to go through some of the most common irritations and how to deal with them.

Ants

Ants love nectar almost as much as hummingbirds do, so if you have sources of nectar around (and you will out of necessity), chances are you're going to struggle with ants. That's the bad news, but the good news is that they're relatively easy to deal with as a pest.

Ants only have one way of transportation, crawling. So how do you stop ants from being annoying in your garden? You blockade their paths, or make the paths unattractive enough that they won't bother.

This will mainly surround your feeder. Some feeders come with a built in pest repelling moat like ring of water that makes it impossible for the ants to get to the nectar, but others will require a bit more creativity. If you're on your own for creating an obstacle, try coating a section of the pole that holds your feeder in petroleum jelly or cooking olive oil. This will dry out over time, and should be reapplied about once a week, but represents an extremely easy way to deal with ants.

Just one word of caution: DO NOT spread this substance on the feeders themselves. This could result in the hummingbirds feathers getting caught in it, and end up harming the creatures you're trying to protect! Instead, coat only the pole that holds the feeder up (or that it hangs from, depending on your feeder).

Bats

This is admittedly somewhat of a regional problem, but still bears addressing. If you do live in a region where bats are around, it can lead to your feeder getting drained overnight. While you sleep, bats will come in and take the sustenance. Now, not everyone is bothered by this, it may just mean a few more refills, but if it's a problem for you, consider taking your feeder down at night.

This will provide no sustenance for the bats, and save it all for the hummers, but does require bringing it in and out of the house every day (which in and of itself can be a nuisance). After all, bats are nighttime pollinators that benefit from the food for hummingbirds too.

Bees & Beyond

Unlike ants, bees (and several other types of insect) can fly and love nectar, so they represent a different type of challenge.

This again will surround your feeder. Some feeders come equipped with bee guards, but this can deter hummingbirds as well as the bugs. A better solution is to take your feeder inside for about a week. This will encourage the bees to move on, and they'll find another food source, leaving yours free to start taking care of the birds again.

Other Birds

Finches, orioles, woodpeckers... these are just three types of potential other birds that your hummingbird feeder may attract. The problem here is that they can start to stop the hummingbirds from feeding, destroying the original purpose of the feeder. The best solution is to provide extra feeders with sugar water or jelly, to allow a few for these other birds and a few for the hummers.

Other Animals

On top of the risk of other types of birds being attracted to your feeder, you may also find racoons and squirrels playing with it. This can be a particular problem because these creatures tend not only to drink the sugar water, but also to break the feeders.

If you're having a problem with small animals, try hanging the feeder with fishing line. This won't provide enough of a hold for squirrels or racoons, but will still have enough strength to hold up the feeder. Another possible solution is to provide baffles on the hangers or the poles to stop them from reaching the feeder, but this can still result in them climbing up and around it frequently enough to be annoying.

Species of Hummingbird

We've already discussed the fact that there are hundreds of species of hummingbird. To that end, there's no way that one guide is going to capture them all (not unless it does absolutely nothing else!). With that in mind, we selected some of the most commonly spotted North American hummingbird species to focus on. This chapter is going to overview a bit about who the species is, and how to tell if you're looking at one, as well as a bit about their behaviour.

Ready to learn more about hummingbirds than most people will probably ever know? Then here we go!

Buff-bellied Hummingbird

Formally known as? Amazilia Yucatanensis

Call sounds like? Complicated to characterize, a full song with rises and falls, distinctive notes, and trills.

Distinctive features
- Their call
- Red beak that's tipped in black

Most likely to spot them? Along the coast of Texas.

A bit about the bird

This mid-sized hummer measures in at 4 ½ inches. It's cute, it's distinctly colored, and it has a unique song – what more could bird watchers ask for?

They aren't as territorial as some of the other species, and males often allow females to feed in their regions. That being said, other males are still thoroughly unwelcome, and will be chased extensively if they make the mistake of invading.

While the buff-bellies song is enjoyable, it mostly only comes but once a year – mating season (April-November). The birds mating is initiated by a male performing a J flight pattern in front of available females. They then mate and the females depart to nest (this is a common trend amongst hummers).

For their part, females build the nests out of thistle down, cattle hair, and vegetable fibres, and coated in bark and lichen. They favour anacahuita, hackberry, and willow trees, as it allows for a higher vantage point of at least three feet off of the ground.

The migration of buff bellies does not start until relatively late in the year, in late autumn, but that may be because they simply don't have as much territory to cover. These hummers prefer coastal Mexico when they're ready to travel, and wait out the winter there.

One odd thing about the migration patterns of buff bellies? Some actually migrate north on the Gulf Coast rather than south! Little is known about why this occurs, but it represents a unique fact about the bird.

Black-Chinned Hummingbird

Formally known as? Archilochus Alexandri

Call sounds like? Tchew

Distinctive features

- Dark coloring. They almost look black at first glance, but are actually a deep shade of purple.
- Flight pattern follows a U shape
- They tail pump while they're hovering over a spot

Most likely to spot them? Western States.

A bit about the bird

The Archilochus Alexandri shows strong preference for isolation, making its home out in the desert and along the West coast. They will venture into the suburbs, and are easily recognized for their unique coloring and distinctive call.

Their territories start getting selected in early March, and once set are fairly firm. This species flies in a U shape to express distress with intruders. If interested in mating, a male will follow a female out of his territory, where they will then breed and she can make her way back to her prepared nest.

Their nests tend to be composed of flowers, bark, lichens, stamen, and are often hung over water (though not always).

In terms of their migration season, Archilochus Alexandri begins the journey in late summer, migrating to warm and sunny Mexico, or Southeastern States, for the winter.

Ruby-Throated Hummingbird

Formally known as? Arichilochus Colubris

Call sounds like? Tchew (very soft though)

Distinctive features

- Location: They are the dominant species throughout Eastern North America
- Size: 3 ¼ inch, extremely tiny

Most likely to spot them? Along the East coast of North America

A bit about the bird

There are few species of hummers as tiny as the ruby-throated, as its 3 ¼ inches represents one of the smallest birds in North America.

That being said, Arichilochus Colubris are still extremely territorial. They will pursue and even fight other hummers for food and territory, and may even behave aggressively with human beings if they feel their territory is being encroached upon. The males do make a notable exception for females of their species, but this is likely so they can stay within territory to mate.

Once mated, females build their nests out of twigs and leaves, their nests too are particularly known for their small (walnut level) size. This typically begins in March, leaving plenty of time for the young offspring to come up and prepare for the long migration south. That being said, these birds are so ingrained in their migration patterns, that a late return can postpone the breeding season as late as June without issue.

Their migration begins in the early fall (sometimes late summer), and is often quite a sight in and of itself. Ruby throats seem to enjoy travelling in large groups, and make regularly favored stops along the way each year, making them a prime target for birdwatchers. Ultimately, they head to southern Mexico, and even parts of Costa Rica – this bird really does not like the cold.

Anna's Hummingbird

Formally known as? Calypte anna

Call sounds like? Tzip

Distinctive features

- Rose-red coloring in the gorget and atop the crown
- Has been known to sing from perches regularly

Most likely to spot them? Along the Pacific Coast, particularly in California, but ranging all the way up to British Columbia (and down to Arizona).

A bit about the bird

Calypte anna are among the bigger hummingbirds. Their four inch wonders are known for their adaptability, surviving humanity settling along their homestead with apparent ease. They are extremely territorial, as many hummers are, and can often be seen putting on amusing displays of song from exposed branches and perches (this of course, is the males).

Females on the other hand act as the gatherers, flitting along and gathering food and necessary nesting supplies before settling down. Interestingly, even territorial male Calypte anna will allow foreign females into their territory – so long as they're out on a supply run as it were.

The nests are primarily composed of spider webs and lichen, with some feathers for cushion to keep the little ones secure. They favor oak, but primarily any place they can keep hidden from the nearby human eyes.

Interestingly, Calypte anna is one of the few species that doesn't really migrate. Instead, they develop a specific breeding range, and nest nearby, not having to worry about the cold on the sunny shores of California. They use the time to breed, and begin late fall to take advantage of the tropical winter weather.

Costa's Hummingbird

Formally known as? Calypte Costae

Call sounds like? A very high pitched call, often known to sound like tik noise.

Distinctive features
- Coloring – specifically a deep violet crown and gorget
- Noisy bird, likes to chatter between the males
- Size – 3 ½ inches

Most likely to spot them? Arizona, southern California – deserts.

A bit about the bird

The male hummingbirds are often the most colorful, and this is seldom more true as with Calypte Costae. The males offer a brilliant display of purple, where the females are gray and green.

Their size too is distinctive, as this is another tiny variety of hummingbird, Calypte Costae measures up to about 3 ½ inches.

The Costa hummer is also particularly territorial, and males can regularly be seen policing their areas with a series of tiks and dives. They will often chase intruders off, occasionally flying side by side to ensure compliance.

The mating season of the Costa begins typically around February, in alliance with the arrival of flowers. These hummingbirds come together to breed, and then the females take off to lay eggs.

The females are particularly bold too, and can often be seen nesting close to human beings. Their nests too are different, in that they use a little bit of everything rather than just a few supplies (bark, bud scales, lichen, string, spider web, etc.)

The birds have picked a relatively warm region to settle, so they don't often need to migrate, but they do move around once the young grow up. The female will chase them away after a few days of fledging to find their own territory as she will most likely breed again in the same area.

Broad-Billed Hummingbird

Formally known as? Cynanthus Latirostris

Call sounds like? Raspy je-dit

Distinctive features

- Coloring: They have a distinctive combination of a red bill and a dark green coat (for males).

Most likely to spot them? Southeast Arizona, New Mexico, and southwest Mexico

A bit about the bird

This species of hummer is particularly known for its unique coloring. It can be found primarily in deserts and wooded areas, and makes quite a splash with its blue throat and green coat, finished by a red bill. The colors of course are more distinct with the males, but the females still have the distinctive je-dit call that they have become known for.

Mating rituals are relatively simply performed, the male need only fly while revving his wings in an easy pendulum. Once mating occurs, the female takes to the nest she has prepared to lay her eggs. Their nests are primarily composed of grass, plant down, and spider webs, though they are often camouflaged with bark or leaves.

Interestingly, this hummer nests at near ground level, rare for something so tiny. They seem to compensate for the apparent risk by occasionally nesting in poison ivy.

Magnificent Hummingbird

Formally known as? Eugenes Fulgens

Call sounds like? Chirp

Distinctive features

- Dark coloring
- Size – they are huge at 5 ¼ inches

Most likely to spot them? Southern Arizona, New Mexico, and western Texas.

A bit about the bird

Eugenes Fulgens is a big hummingbird, a really big hummingbird. While there are larger birds in the world on a species level, this hummer measures in at the absolute top of the hummer scale of size.

As the name suggests, they are utterly beautiful, almost appearing to glitter with their mix of dark blues, greens, and blacks. As always, the female is a more subtle hue, coming in with more grays and greens, but even she is distinctive for her size.

They typically mate, and females take the resulting eggs off to spider web and lichen nests, always highly elevated.

This particular species does migrate, often heading down to Mexico till the cold abates.

Blue-Throated Hummingbird

Formally known as? Lampornis Clemencia

Call sounds like? Seek (in a very high pitch)

Distinctive features

- Blue throat, white eyes, white tail
- Size and aggressive nature

Most likely to spot them? Southern States (think Arizona, New Mexico, and Texas).

A bit about the bird

This is probably one of the most aggressive varieties of hummingbird. Blue throat hummers often set up ambush attacks at feeders for other birds, and certainly require their own feeder if they've invaded your yard.

They settle primarily in the regions above, favoring areas of high elevation with an open nature (perhaps because of how aggressive they are).

Bluebird's mating rituals are something of a mystery, though females do nest from April to mid-July. Females form the nest out of somewhat rougher materials, ranging from moss and stems, to straw and oak catkins. That being said, the inside is still extremely softly lined with plant down.

The bird will migrate to Mexico for the winter, but a few stop as north as Arizona.

Allen's Hummingbird

Formally known as? Selasphorus Sasin

Call sounds like? Chp, chp, chp

Recognizable features

- Distinctive green back
- Flight pattern follows a J shape

Most likely to spot them? Along the Pacific coast, ranging from southern California all the way up to southwestern Oregon.

A bit about the bird

Selasphorus sasin range on the tinier side of the hummingbird family, measuring in at 3 ¼ inches on average. They have become known for their striking similarity to the rufous hummingbird, but show their true colours with their distinctive green backsides.

Their mating season begins in the fall, and is characterized by an increase in males flying that famous J and chp, chping just a little more determinedly to attract their mates. Once successfully bred, females retreat to a distance away from the otherwise territorial males, often nesting in an oak tree.

Their nests are often composed of the usual, but also have been known to include animal hair, flowers, and occasionally spider silk. It makes a warm, bark lined home for the new birds to grow for their long flight along the Pacific Coast.

Broad-Tailed Hummingbird

Formally known as? Selasphorus Platycerus

Call sounds like? Chirping.

Distinctive features

- Display dive that occurs during territory claiming and mating activities.
- Wings make an almost whistling noise themselves

Most likely to spot them? High up in the Rocky Mountains of Colorado

A bit about the bird

The Selasphorus Platycerus is so predictably found in the Rockies it's almost a tourist attraction. If you put out a feeder in the area, you will see the broad tailed hummingbird.

They settle by first letting the male stake territorial claims. Once all the males have finished display diving to claim their territories, they enforce them.

The mating ritual is brief, but effective. And then starts the nesting season. Unsurprisingly, the females nest far from the territories of the males in play, and coat them in willows and cottonwood, coated in bark and grass. This occurs sometime around the spring, giving the new younglings plenty of time to learn all that they need before migration season.

These hummers migrate in the late summer, and head down to Mexico typically for the winter.

Rufous Hummingbird

Formally known as? Selasphorus rufus

Call sounds like? Chp, chp, chp

Distinctive features

- Aggressive nature
- Coloring – primarily hues of brown in the males, with green in the females
- Lack of fear of cold regions

Most likely to spot them? Alaska, the Pacific Northwest, or the Rockies.

A bit about the bird

The rufous hummer is a notoriously aggressive, northern dwelling breed of hummingbird. Their colors are primarily hues of brown in the males, but females (as often) display more greens than browns.

Though both of the sexes are quite noisy, it is the males who are most territorial, often marking their territories out with a distinct J or O shaped flight pattern. Females are welcome amongst male territories, primarily to give the males more chances to impress them.

Once mating has occurred (spring time) the female lays her eggs in a soft nest of plant down and cobwebs, the outside protected by some bark, lichens, and moss.

On top of being known for being dominant, they are also known for their migration. These birds start migrating in early summer – early fall at the latest, perhaps because their environments are already cold, and they travel in large numbers as they do. They tend to winter in Mexico, but have also been spotted in the southeastern US.

Calliope Hummingbird

Formally known as? Stellula Calliope

Call sounds like? Tik, and males can also go Tz

Distinctive features

- Coloring (purple gorget plumes)
- Size (very very small)

Most likely to spot them? The Rocky Mountains.

A bit about the bird

The Calliope hummer is known for two primary things: its colors and its size. These birds have a striking streak of purple along the gorget that often stands out, particularly evident in the males of the species. Stellula calliope is by far the smallest hummingbird in North America. Its 3 ¼ inches are so tiny in fact, that it may well be the tiniest species of bird period – of any family!

Don't let their size fool you though, this little hummer is often seen aggressively pursuing other, bigger species.

Mating season kicks off with a series of male flight patterns in the shape of a U, along with their special mating call, in the hopes of finding that one special other bird. Once settled, the female then goes off to nest along the edge of a field of alder or willow, producing a nest of bark, leaves, and moss.

As we know, hummers hate the cold, and the fact that Calliope's prefer the mountains as their normal habitat necessitates a migration pattern. They typically begin migrating mid-late summer, and tend to cluster in the southeastern US and in Mexico (a popular hummer destination, no doubt!).

Unexpected Sightings

Each of the species above has a favored region that it's known to be found in, but this does not mean that's always where it is. Hummers tend to like to surprise us, and have often been spotted well outside their expected regions.

Bird sightings you might not expect

- Amazilia Beryllina (the Berylline hummer)
- Amazilia Rutila (the Cinnamon hummer)
- Amazilia Violiceps (the Violet Crowned hummer) has been seen in southeastern Arizona, and southwestern New Mexico.
- Anthracothorax Prevostii (Green breasted mango)
- Calliphlox Evelynae (the Bahama woodstar)
- Calothorax Lucifer (the Lucifer hummer) occasionally has been spotted breeding in southeastern Arizona, southwestern New Mexico, and western Texas.
- Colibri Thalassinus (the Green Violet Ear hummer) has been seen going from Southern Mexico to northern areas of South America, but also in Texas.
- Helimaster Constantii (the Plain capped star throat)
- Hylocharis Leuctis (the White Eared hummer) are regularly spotted in southern Arizona, with no site of their nests.
- Hylocharis Xantussi

These are just a few of the species that make regular trips outside of their region, for reasons we don't often understand. There are a myriad more of examples to be provided, with hummers unexpectedly popping up all over North America.

If you spot a hummer you aren't sure should be there, report it to your local bird watching club or ornithological society. Others enjoy sharing in the rarities and success stories, so feel free to connect!

Frequently Asked Questions about Hummingbirds

There are a lot of questions people have asked over the years, but this chapter is going to review some of the most commonly asked and answered ones.

Do hummingbirds change color? While hummers do not actually change color, the gorget is often caught by different angles of the light. Due to the subtle hues of some of our favorite breeds, hummers often give off different shades at different times, sometimes even appearing completely dark!

Do hummingbirds love red? It does seem that hummers enjoy red, though it's not entirely clear as to why. They will go to flowers and such of any color, and they will still find feeders without food dye (don't put it in), but red does seem to attract their attention. Researchers have speculated that perhaps red stands out in their fields of vision, or have developed as an evolutionary signal for food.

How long does migration take? This depends on the species, as different hummers are headed different places and leave at different times, so it's very hard to specify. That being said, hummingbirds have been known to frequent favorite stops, so don't be surprised if you wind up able to predict when you might spot certain ones based on the season.

Where do hummingbirds sleep? Hummers are experts at finding tiny little pockets of shelter. They puff themselves out and sleep often in trees or shrubs.

Is hummingbird overdependence on feeders a risk? Hummingbirds will never develop a dependency issue on a feeder because, although it helps, it is not their only source of nutrition. They still seek out nectar from flowers, regardless of whether they are regularly feeding or not.

When should feeders be removed? Hummers are going to migrate regardless of the presence of feeders. You should only really need to take down your feeder if you're having a problem with bats, or if you live in an area where you need to take it down for the winter to prevent damage to it.

Why are hummingbirds fighting in my yard? Hummingbirds are notoriously territorial, and sometimes aggressive. If there are hummers fighting, chances are you need to get one or more additional feeders, hopefully hung out of sight of one another, to allow the competing birds to all eat.

Why did my hummers leave? Hummers will leave an area if they are migrating, if they've found a different way to get food more effectively, or if they're just passing through an area. It's nothing to be concerned about, more will come.

Why doesn't Hawaii have hummingbirds? Hummingbirds are primarily a Western bird, preferring coastal regions of North America to entirely tropical habitats.

Can any other type of bird hover like hummers do? No, belted kingfishers, American kestrels, and certain species of hawk have all been known to hover while pursuing prey. That being said, hummingbirds are known for their distinct hovering, as they do it more frequently and more gracefully than other birds. Hummers are also the only birds that can fly backwards and upside down.

Does feeding hummingbirds prevent their migration?

Hummingbirds do enjoy being fed, and may enjoy frequenting the same places, but being fed late into the season is not going to change their migration patterns. The reality of it is that feeders can only help so much, and that their plant diet dictates when they leave the area.

Once they've started to leave, nothing is going to stop this process. If they wait longer than a few days, they risk death, so the only factors that would lead them to do this would be illness or needing to stock up on food. There is no harm in feeding hummingbirds, it will not stop their migration.

We hope you've enjoyed reading, and feel free to do further research if you still have questions after reading it! Enjoy your brand new hobby, and have fun spotting the hummers!

Sign up to AttractingWildBirds.com newsletter to get strategies for attracting wild birds to your backyard, bird watching tips, and more delivered to your inbox!

www.attractingwildbirds.com